West Virginia Fish Species
Game Fish & Panfish

Billy Grinslott – Kinsey Marie Books

ISBN - 9781968228484

Redear sunfish are known for their red or orange-edged gill flaps. They are a type of sunfish that thrive in warm, quiet waters, feeding primarily on mollusks and snails, and can grow up to 12 inches and weigh as much as 2 pounds. They are also known as shellcracker, due to their diet and the way they crush shells. The redear sunfish will thrive in most warm-water lakes and streams.

The Flier is a small, sunfish known for its olive-green color, rows of dark spots, and a dark teardrop or streak below its eye, with large dorsal and anal fins. It inhabits slow-moving, clear waters in the Southern U.S. coastal plains and Mississippi river basin. They feed on insects, snails, worms, leeches, crustaceans, and small fish, also some phytoplankton.

The bluegill also considered a sunfish is the most popular fish to fish for. They are called pan fish because they are about the size of a frying pan. Bluegills love to eat insects and bugs. They have good vision and rely on their keen eyesight to feed. Three types in this group are the Bluegill, Sunfish, and Pumpkinseed.

The Redbreast sunfish has a red-yellow chest and belly with rusty brown spots on their body. The species is known for its distinctive grunting vocalizations, which are produced by grinding their teeth together. Redbreast sunfish can survive in oxygen-poor environments by using their gills to extract oxygen from air bubbles trapped in aquatic vegetation.

The Green Sunfish is blue green in color. It has yellow flecks on both its scales and some parts of its sides. The Green Sunfish also has broken blue stripes which is why some people confuse it with the Bluegill. Green Sunfish are very adaptable. They can live in any body of water that has vegetation or weeds. Green sunfish are opportunistic feeders, consuming insects, small fish, and other invertebrates.

The Pumpkinseed is also known as pond perch, sun perch, and punky's sunfish. It can be found in numerous lakes, ponds, and rivers. It is their body shape resembling the seed of a pumpkin, that inspired their name. Pumpkinseed sunfish have speckles on their orangish colored sides and back, with a yellow to orange belly and chest. They are active during the day and rest at night near the bottom or in shelter areas.

The Rock Bass is not actually a bass but a member of the sunfish family. They are often called red eye or goggle eye due to their distinctive bright red eyes. The biggest Rock Bass ever caught on record weighs about three pounds and was a little over one foot long. Rock bass prefer waters with rocky vegetated areas, that's how they got their name.

The Warmouth is a member of the Rock Bass, Green Sunfish and Bluegill family. They can survive in low oxygen environments while other fish cannot. Warmouth can thrive in muddy water, when other fish can't. Warmouth are often confused with rock bass. The difference between the two is in the anal fin: warmouth have three spines on the anal fin ray and rock bass have six spines.

Longear sunfish are small, thin-bodied fish with a unique long ear flap on their gill cover, that how they got their name long ear. They are often mistaken for a pumpkinseed. They have an olive to rusty-brown back, a bright orange belly. They typically reach a length of 4.5 inches. They are mostly active during the day and inactive at night.

The two most famous perches are the common perch and the yellow perch. The yellow perch has a brilliant greenish yellow color with orange fins. The yellow perch is the biggest one and can grow to a size of 18 inches. It's also known as the jumbo perch. The other type of perch is the white perch. The biggest yellow perch caught in West Virginia, by weight, is 2.04 pounds.

White perch grow seven to ten inches in length and rarely weigh more than one pound. They have a silvery body with faint lines on the sides. The white perch is an opportunistic feeder. Young feed primarily on zooplankton and adults feed on aquatic insect larvae, minnows and fish eggs. White Perch is a euryhaline species, inhabiting fresh, brackish and coastal waters. The biggest White Perch caught in West Virginia is a 2-pound, 1-ounce fish.

There are two main types of crapples. The white crapple and the black crappie. They are also members of the sunfish family. The difference between the white and black crappie is one has dark spots and the other has dark lines and is lighter in color. The white crappie has six dorsal fin spines, whereas the black crappie has eight dorsal fin spines. The white crappie can grow bigger and more of the bigger white crappie are caught in North America. The biggest crappie caught in West Virginia for weight is 3.6 pounds.

Bowfins can breathe both air and water, putting them at an advantage in low-oxygen waters. Bowfins are often described as prehistoric relics. This is because species can be traced to fossils from the Cretaceous, Eocene and Jurassic period. The biggest bowfin caught in West Virginia, setting a new state weight record, was a 10.60-pound fish.

There are few different species of Gar, the Longnose gar, Short nose and Alligator gar. The Long Nose Gar got its name because of its long mouth that looks like an alligator's mouth. The alligator gar is one of the biggest freshwater fish growing up to 10 feet long. The world record for a catch was set at 327 pounds. The biggest longnose gar caught in West Virginia was a record-breaking 53.62-inch fish.

Redhorse are large, bottom-feeding freshwater sucker fish known for their reddish fins, and molar-like throat teeth that they use to crush mollusks. They inhabit in clear rivers with gravelly bottoms, where they feed on insects and detritus. They spawn in spring, often migrating upstream. They are popular with anglers for their strong fight, when catching them in swift currents. They can grow to around 18 pounds and 30 inches long.

Male freshwater drum make a rumbling or grunting sound by contracting muscles along their air bladder walls. They have large, ivory-like ear bones that can be up to an inch in diameter, which Native Americans used as necklaces or bracelets and sometimes referred to as the lucky stones. Freshwater drum are primarily bottom feeders, spending much of their time near the bottom of lakes and rivers in search of food. The biggest freshwater drum caught in West Virginia weighed 27.88 pounds.

Carp have long been an important food fish to humans. Carp are bottom feeders for the most part and their mouth is made like a suction cup, so they can suck food off the bottom. Carp are good for a lake because they help clean the bottom of the lake. Carp are introduced for aquatic vegetation control and can grow very large. The biggest Common Carp caught in West Virginia weighed 47 pounds.

The black, brown and yellow bullhead are part of the catfish family. They usually only grow to about 10 inches long. They use their whiskers to help find food. The bullhead is the most common member of the catfish family. Bullheads live in the water containing low oxygen levels. They can survive on low oxygen areas, where other fish can't. The biggest bullhead caught in West Virginia is a 22.75-inch, 6.1-pound fish.

White catfish are interesting because they are smaller than other common catfish species like channel catfish, they have a wider head and lack the black spots of channel catfish. White catfish are the smallest of the large North American catfish species. The White catfish has white chin barbells, which distinguish it from other species. There are four pairs of barbels, whiskers around the mouth, two on the chin, one at the angle of the mouth, and one behind the nostril.

Flathead Catfish, their body is wide but flattened and very low in height. Both eyes are on the top of the flattened head, giving excellent vision to see upward. Flathead catfish live mainly in large bodies of water like big rivers and reservoirs. They prefer deep pools of water. The biggest Flathead Catfish ever caught in West Virginia weighed 70 pounds.

The Channel Catfish are the most fished catfish species with around 8 million anglers fishing for them per year. Channel catfish have taste buds all over their body, making them highly sensitive to the taste and smell of food. They also have barbels (whiskers) around their mouths, which are used for sensing and tasting food. They use sound waves to communicate with each other. They can also produce alarm substances to warn other catfish of danger. The biggest Channel Catfish caught in West Virginia weighed 46.70 pounds.

Blue catfish are known for their size, reaching over 100 pounds. Blue catfish, like other catfish, lack scales and have smooth skin. They have barbels (whiskers) around their mouths, which are used for sensing and tasting food. They are generally slate blue on the back and silvery/white on the underside. The biggest blue catfish caught in West Virginia, setting the current weight record, was a massive 69.45-pound fish.

White Bass or striped bass range in color from a silvery white to a pale green. Their backs are mostly black, while their sides and belly are pale with stripes running along them. White Bass are related to Striped Bass and sometimes called wipers. The biggest White Bass caught in West Virginia weighed 4.56 pounds.

The Hybrid Striped Bass is a cross between a male White Bass and a female Striped Bass, known for its broken stripes, deep body, and excellent fighting ability. It's a favorite game fish in many freshwater reservoirs, prized for its aggressive nature, often caught with spoons, jigs, or live bait, especially in cooler months. They are sterile and do not reproduce naturally, so they are stocked in lakes and rivers by state hatcheries. They can grow to significant sizes, often reaching several pounds within three years. The biggest Hybrid Striped Bass (Wiper) caught in West Virginia weighed 16.75 pounds.

Striped bass are often called Stripers. Striped bass live in both salt and fresh water. Striped bass have very sensitive eyes and will seek deep water when the sun is out. Striped bass have a preferred water temperature range of from 55° F to 68° F, and swim to find water of these temperatures. White Bass are related to Striped Bass and have lighter stripes on their sides. The biggest striped bass caught in West Virginia was a 45.70-pound fish.

Spotted bass have rows of dark spots on their sides and an iridescent green pattern along their back. Spotted bass are also known as Kentucky's or redeye bass. They are a popular game fish, often mistaken for largemouth bass, but they have subtle differences like a a smaller mouth. They are known for their aggressive nature and tendency to school together. They also prefer rocky bottoms and being in deeper water compared to other bass who like shallow water. The biggest Spotted Bass in West Virginia weighed 4.77 pounds.

The largemouth bass is the most sought-after bass in North America. Largemouth bass live in just about every lake in North America. They have great hearing and can hear a crayfish crawling on the bottom of the lake. The biggest largemouth bass by weight in West Virginia is 12.28 pounds.

Smallmouth bass have a smaller mouth than the largemouth bass. They also have different markings and are lighter in color. They don't live in most lakes because they prefer living in colder water. They are typically found in the northern states in America because the water is cooler. The current world record smallmouth is an 11-pound, 15-ounce fish caught in Dale Hollow Lake. The biggest smallmouth bass caught in West Virginia by weight is 9.75 pounds.

Paddlefish are among the oldest surviving fish species in North America, dating back to about 125 million years ago. Their most distinctive feature is their long, flat, paddle-shaped snout, which helps them detect and locate tiny aquatic creatures. Paddlefish are true bottom-dwelling creatures, that are hard to catch and can grow to weigh over 160 pounds.

Shovelnose Sturgeons have sharp spines on their back, so be careful when handling them. Instead of scales, sturgeon skin is covered in bony plates called scutes, which can be very sharp on young sturgeon. Sturgeons have been around since the dinosaur days. Sturgeons mostly live in large, freshwater lakes and rivers. Their average lifespan is 50 to 60 years. The most notable catch in West Virginia was a 10-foot White Sturgeon.

The sauger is part of the walleye family. There are 2 different types of saugers. The normal sauger and the suageye. The saugeye is a mix of the sauger and walleye. The suageye have white eyes just like the walleye. The sauger and suageye are smaller than the walleye. Saugers are more likely to be found in large rivers with deep pools but are also found in lakes. The biggest sauger caught in West Virginia by weight is 5.06 pounds.

The walleye got its name because of its white looking eyes. Their eyes collect light, even in low light conditions. This means they can see in the dark. Because they can see in the dark, they mostly feed at night. During the daytime their eyes are very sensitive, so they usually head for deeper water or shady places. Walleye like to live in cooler water and are normally found in the upper part of North America. The biggest walleye caught in West Virginia weighed 18.97 pounds

Pickerel, also called pike, look like northern pike, but they are not. The Pike is larger in size than the Pickerel. The Pickerel has more spots than the Pike, but the Pike has spots on its fins and pickerel don't. The Pickerel has a dark bar beneath their eyes and northern pike don't. There are 2 types of Pickerel, Chain Pickerel, and Redfin Pickerel. The biggest Chain Pickerel caught in West Virginia by weight was 6.19 pounds.

The Northern Pike is one of the most sought-after fish for anglers. It got its name because it likes to live in cooler water mainly in the northern states of North America. The northern pike is a very aggressive predator. They don't like to live in groups with other fish, they are very territorial and like to live alone. Their behavior is closely affected by weather conditions. The biggest Northern Pike caught in West Virginia weighed 22.06 pounds, measured 42.6 inches long.

The muskellunge called the Musky or Muskie for short is one of the biggest game fish in freshwater lakes. They are hard to catch, they say it takes a thousand casts to catch one. They're stocked and sought by anglers in these connected cool-water river systems. Muskellunge (Muskie) are primarily found in the western mountain rivers like the New, Nolichucky, and French Broad Rivers, and reservoirs such as Fontana and Lake Adger and Hiwassee. The biggest muskellunge caught in West Virginia measured 55.0625 inches long and weighed 51 pounds.

The tiger muskie is a cross between the northern pike and muskie. They grow larger and faster than normal muskies and northern pikes. The tiger muskie got its name because it has tiger like stripes. Tiger Muskies are very rare and hard to catch. Tiger muskie have been stocked in several locations. The biggest Tiger Muskie caught in West Virginia weighed 36 pounds, 8 ounces.

Tiger trout are known for their aggressive nature and awesome looking tiger-like stripes. Tiger trout are not naturally occurring in the wild, but rather a hybrid created by mixing a female brown trout with a male brook trout. They are stocked in lakes and rivers. Their striking appearance with tiger-like stripes and patterns, makes them easily recognizable. They are known to grow faster than their parent species. The biggest tiger trout by weight in West Virginia is 12.55 pounds.

Brown trout can live up to 20 years. Brown exhibits a variety of colors and spotting patterns, with red spots surrounded by blue halos and black spots being common. Brown trout have higher tolerance for warmer waters than either the brook or rainbow trout. Brown trout can be found on almost every continent except Antarctica. The biggest brown trout caught in West Virginia by weight is 16 pounds.

Mature Golden trout have a deep olive-green back that fades to bright gold on the sides, a vibrant red-orange lateral line, and black speckles near the tail. Golden trout are native to the remote waters at elevations of 6,000 to 10,000 feet. Golden trout, typically average 6 to 12 inches in length. The biggest Golden Trout (Golden Rainbow Trout) caught in West Virginia weighed 9.72 pounds.

Brook trout are characterized by their olive-green bodies with pale, worm-like markings, red spots with bluish halos, and orange-red fins with white and black edges. They can grow up to 12 inches in length. Brook trout are cold-water fish that prefer clean, clear, and cold streams, lakes, and ponds. The biggest Brook Trout caught in West Virginia weighed 7.64 pounds and measured 23.5 inches long.

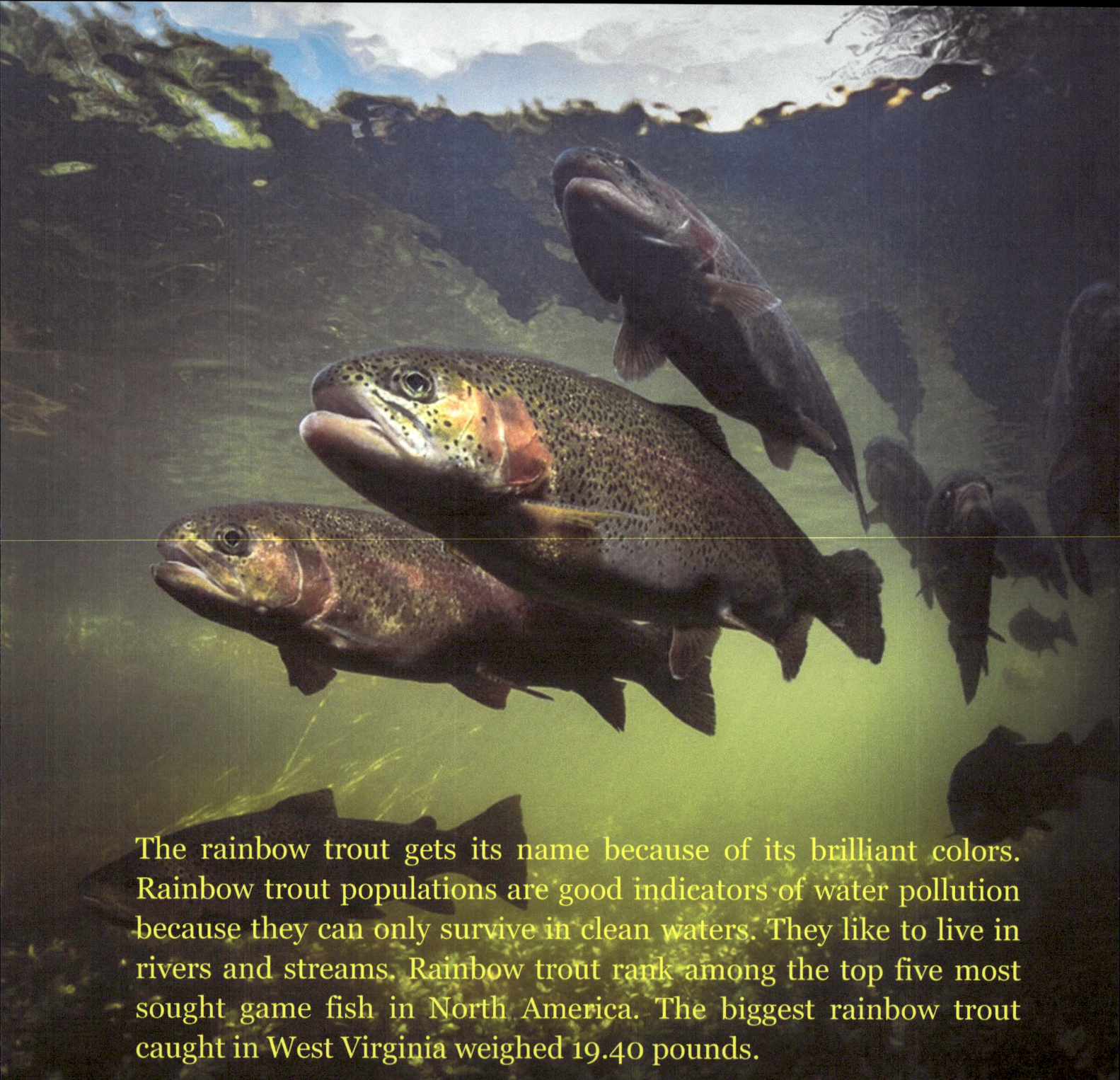

The rainbow trout gets its name because of its brilliant colors. Rainbow trout populations are good indicators of water pollution because they can only survive in clean waters. They like to live in rivers and streams. Rainbow trout rank among the top five most sought game fish in North America. The biggest rainbow trout caught in West Virginia weighed 19.40 pounds.

Interesting Fish Facts in West Virginia.

1 – The native Brook Trout is West Virginia's state freshwater fish, thriving in cold water mountain streams.

2 - West Virginia's streams and rivers host Over 178 Species of fish, from tiny darters to large predators, across 24 families.

3 - Popular game fish include Largemouth Bass, Smallmouth Bass, and Black Crappie.

4 - The biggest freshwater fish ever caught in West Virginia by weight is a 71.69-pound Grass Carp

5 - The smallest freshwater fish caught in West Virginia is likely the Least Killifish, only 2 inches long.

6 - Species like Channel and Blue Catfish lack scales and use "whiskers" (barbels) with taste buds to find food on the bottom.

7 - Largemouth Bass are a popular target for anglers, with rare genetic golden variants found.

8 - A 70-pound Flathead Catfish holds a state record, caught in the Kanawha River.

Author Page

Billy Grinslott – Kinsey Marie Books

ISBN – 9781968228484

Thanks

www.ingramcontent.com/pod-product-compliance
Lightning Source LLC
Chambersburg PA
CBHW060849270326
41934CB00002B/57